STRANGE UNSOLVED MYSTERIES

MYSTERIES OF SPACE & THE UNIVERSE

Strange, Unsolved Mysteries from Tor books

Mysteries of Ships and Planes
Monsters, Strange Dreams, and UFOs
Mysteries of Bizarre Animals and Freaks of Nature
Mysteries of People and Places
Ghosts, Hauntings and Mysterious Happenings
Mysteries of Space and the Universe

STRANGE UNSOLVED MYSTERIES

MYSTERIES OF SPACE and THE UNIVERSE

PHYLLIS RAYBIN EMERT
Illustrated by JAEL

A TOM DOHERTY ASSOCIATES BOOK
NEW YORK

MYSTERIES OF SPACE AND THE UNIVERSE

Copyright © 1994 by RGA Publishing Group, Inc.

Cover art and interior illustrations by Jael

A Tor Book
Published by Tom Doherty Associates, Inc.
175 Fifth Avenue
New York, N.Y. 10010

Tor® is a registered trademark of Tom Doherty Associates, Inc.

ISBN: 0-812-53631-2

First edition: September 1994

Printed in the United States of America

0 9 8 7 6 5 4 3 2 1

In memory of Matthew Steven Kerkstra

Contents

The Speed of Light   1
The Future of the Sun   5
One Genuine UFO   9
Deadly Collision   14
Climate Catastrophes   19
Incidents in New Mexico   23
Tunnels of Blackness   30
Planet X   35
Mysterious Circles   38
Halley's and Other Comets   44
Through Space and Time   50
Cover-up in Texas   54
Is Anybody Out There?   59

Contents

Messages to the Unknown   64
Red Glowing Disks   70
Life on Mars—Past, Present, Future   74
Nemesis—The Death Star   81
Film at 11   84
Primitive Life-forms   87
Helicopter or Spacecraft?   92
The Search for Life   97
Astronauts and UFOs   102
What the Future Might Hold   106
Glossary   111
Bibliography   117

The Speed of Light

"The sky looks beautiful tonight," declared Jake. "We're lucky there's no cloud cover."

"I've never seen so many stars," exclaimed Holly. "It makes you realize the Earth is just a very small part of the universe."

The stars visible to Jake and Holly are only part of one little section of the Milky Way galaxy in which our solar system is located. There are two or three hundred billion stars in the Milky Way.

Now try to imagine this. There are billions of other galaxies out there, too, all containing billions of stars! So when Holly said Earth is a small part of the universe, she was right. The universe is like a beach and the

Earth is like a single grain of sand on that beach.

When gazing out at the night sky, people don't actually see the stars themselves, they see the light from the stars. It takes time for the light to travel across space. By knowing the speed of light, distances to points throughout the universe can be determined.

Scientists have calculated that the speed of light is 186,282.3959 miles per second. That means that in one second, light travels a little more than 186,282 miles. According to Albert Einstein's theory of relativity, the speed of light is the highest speed limit possible for matter in the universe. It would be impossible to equal or exceed the speed of light because the mass of an object would become infinite (without end), and would therefore take an infinite amount of energy to reach that speed. Although the explanation for this is very complicated, scientists accept it as fact.

It takes light 1.25 seconds to travel from the Moon to the Earth. It takes light 8 minutes and 19 seconds to travel the 93 million miles from the Sun to the Earth. For light to travel from the Sun to Pluto, the most distant planet in our solar system, it takes 11 hours.

The stars are so much farther away from the Earth that scientists use the term "light-year" to measure distances. In one year, light travels just under 6 trillion miles.

The nearest star to Earth (other than the Sun) is called Proxima Centauri. It's 25 trillion miles away, which is equal to 4.27 light-years. This means it takes 4.27 years for light leaving Proxima Centauri to travel across space and reach the eyes of Holly, Jake, or any other stargazer on Earth.

Looking at the stars is like looking into the past. The object, let's say Proxima Centauri, is seen as it was when the light started out, which was 4.27 years ago. That means that the farther out one looks in space, the farther back one is actually looking in time.

The Andromeda galaxy is the nearest galaxy to the Milky Way. It's the most distant object that can be seen on a clear night without a telescope. Andromeda is more than 2 million light-years away, so a stargazer will see it as it was over 2 million years ago.

The most distant objects in the universe are quasars, some of which are 10 to 12 billion light-years away. Quasars are bright and powerful energy sources located at the center of distant galaxies. They can be seen by large telescopes. Just imagine that the light from some of these quasars started traveling in the direction of Earth before our own solar system and Earth itself ever existed. (Our solar system is about 4.6 billion years old.)

On the other hand, by studying and observing quasars, scientists are seeing 10 to 12 billion years into the past. The universe is about 15 billion years old, give or take a billion. So astronomers are seeing galaxies the way they were shortly after the birth of the universe.

Is it possible to look back into the past and see the actual creation of the universe itself? According to the late scientist Isaac Asimov, in his book *Guide to Earth and Space*, it wouldn't be possible by using light, since space was filled with foggy energy in the early days of the universe. But microwaves from the giant explosion that scientists believe once created the universe should be able to reach us.

"Telescopes are able to look farther and farther into the distance," declared Asimov, "and farther and farther into the past." The mystery of the birth of the universe is waiting to be solved by brilliant young astronomers and scientists. One of them could be you!

The Future of the Sun

People take the Sun for granted. It's a necessary part of life on Earth, yet we barely give it a second thought each day. We just assume the Sun will rise each morning and set each night like clockwork, and since mankind has lived on Earth, it has!

Even our vocabulary reflects our feelings about the Sun. Someone with a "sunny" personality is cheerful and happy. People say they want their "place in the sun," which is defined as a favorable position or situation. Lovers sing to each other: "You are the sunshine of my life."

The Sun is everything good about life. It gives the Earth its days and nights, the seasons of each year, heat, energy, and food. It will always be there for us, won't it?

The answer is no. Because it is a star, the Sun will burn out and die. Life on Earth as we know it will end. But all is not lost! Scientists believe mankind can continue to survive by colonizing the outer planets and the space around them. The first step is space colonies in orbit around the Earth, then a colony on the Moon, and finally colonies in the outer solar system.

Scientist Gerard O'Neill of Princeton suggests populating high rotating cylinders several miles long and a few miles in diameter in space. Large numbers of people could live within these cylinders in towns and villages, growing crops and using solar radiation for energy.

Isaac Asimov, in his book *A Choice of Catastrophes*, suggests "redesigning some of the larger satellites of Jupiter, Saturn, Uranus, and Neptune, in order to make them fit for human habitation."

But don't start worrying. Scientists figure the Sun has another 5 to 8 billion years left! For about 4.5 billion years, the Sun has been transferring matter into energy through the use of thermonuclear fusion. The Sun is an average-sized star consisting of three-quarters hydrogen. The immense gravitational pressure and temperature in the outer layers of the Sun cause a nuclear reaction in the center. This reaction (called fusion) changes hydrogen into helium and produces energy in the form of heat and light. The Earth receives only a tiny fraction of the Sun's energy. Most of it goes into outer space beyond the planets.

How hot is the Sun? It's so hot, it's hard to even imagine! Think of a summer day when the temperature hits 100 degrees Fahrenheit, and sipping an ice-cold lemonade is just the thing for the heat. The Sun's surface temperature is about 10,000 degrees Fahrenheit, and its core (or center) is 27 million degrees Fahrenheit!

Eventually, after billions of years, the Sun will use up all of its hydrogen and the core will begin to collapse, unable to resist the gravitational pressure. There will be an increase in density and temperature and the Sun will begin to expand. It will grow bigger and redder, filling up more and more of the sky.

As the Sun slowly moves toward this Red Giant phase, the temperature on Earth will continue to rise. Astrophysicist Icko Iben of the University of Illinois predicts that in about 2 billion years, the winter temperature in what used to be cold and snowy New England will be 90 degrees. The polar ice caps will start to melt, raising the sea level and flooding coastal regions throughout the globe.

The rising temperatures will begin to evaporate, then boil, the oceans. By the time the Sun reaches the peak of its Red Giant phase, it will have destroyed Mercury and Venus. This swollen, red monster, filling up the entire sky, will cause the Earth's crust to melt. Finally, after destroying the Earth and possibly Mars, the Red Giant that was once our Sun will collapse into a dim White Dwarf star, eventually cooling down and dying.

According to Asimov, by the time life becomes impossible on Earth, colonies may already be established on two of Jupiter's satellites, Ganymede and Callisto, and even on Pluto. As the Sun goes through its Red Giant phase, these areas would be warmed by the massive star, but not burned by it.

By the time the sun becomes a White Dwarf, these space colonists might have developed an alternative energy source and be completely independent of the Sun. Perhaps they will even choose to leave the solar system.

There is no way to avoid the death of the Sun, but we have billions of years to prepare for it. The continuation of human life as we know it will be a major challenge of the generations to come.

One Genuine UFO

UFO (unidentified flying object) expert Martin Shough has called it "one of the most remarkable radar-visual sequences on record." The Condon Report for the U.S. Air Force stated it was "the most puzzling and unusual case in the radar-visual files ... the probability that at least one genuine UFO was involved appears to be fairly high." Author G. D. Thayer referred to it as "a mechanical device of unknown origin."

They're all talking about the Bentwaters/Lakenheath UFO sighting, which took place over eastern England on the night of August 13–14, 1956. Read the facts and decide for yourself.

At about 9:30 P.M. radar operators at the Bentwaters Air Base spotted a target on the radar screen moving very fast in a straight line. It vanished off the screen at an estimated speed of about 5,000 miles per hour.

Another group of twelve to fifteen objects was observed on radar to be moving at about 100 miles per hour. These objects seemed to be following three other targets in triangular formation. The objects then merged to form a single blip and stopped moving on the screen. After ten to fifteen minutes, the blip began to move again, then stopped for three to five more minutes, then disappeared from the screen.

Within minutes, another target appeared on the screen at Bentwaters, also estimated to be moving at a speed of more than 5,000 miles per hour. It was too slow to be a meteor and too fast for any known aircraft on Earth.

At 10:55 P.M. another high-speed blip appeared on radar, but this time control tower personnel saw "a bright light passing over the field at terrific speed." At the same time, a C-47 transport pilot saw a bright light "streak under his airplane" at high speed. There were several sightings of this unidentified object as well as radar contact.

Bentwaters notified the air station at Lakenheath to scan their radar screens for the mysterious blips. Soon after, Lakenheath noticed a motionless bright object that suddenly moved at speeds of 600 to 800 miles per hour to another position, then stopped abruptly. The object continued to move at right angles, stopping, then moving again at high speeds.

Around midnight, a decision was made to send a De Havilland Venom night-fighter airplane into the air to intercept the unidentified object that had been under observation.

"I have contact with a bright white light," stated the pilot. The Venom's navigator declared the unmoving object to be "the clearest target I have ever seen on radar."

As the plane closed in on the target, the pilot said, "I've got my guns on him." At that moment, the blip disappeared from radar and suddenly reappeared behind the fighter plane.

"Where did he go? Do you still have him?" asked the pilot.

"Roger," replied Lakenheath. "He got behind you and he's still there."

The pilot of the Venom fighter tried to shake off the object from his tail. In spite of his dive, climb, and turning maneuvers, the unidentified object stayed with the plane at a distance of a quarter mile. The object followed the plane back to its base, and stopped about 10 miles from the airfield. Then it moved off the screen at about 600 miles per hour.

What makes this such an interesting UFO sighting? Ground radars at two different locations, the airborne radar of the Venom fighter, and the pilot's visual sighting all saw this unknown object in the same place at the same time.

It's obvious that something was in the sky that night, and the multiple radar contacts combined with sightings point strongly to the fact that this was an unidentified flying object. The excessive speed and maneuverability of the object could not have been equaled by any aircraft in 1956 or even today (except for the X-15 experimental rocket plane, whose flights lasted only 84 to 180 seconds).

The behavior of the UFO supports the fact that it was controlled by intelligent, reasoning beings. At one point, it even tricked the plane sent to intercept it by using its speed and maneuverability to come up behind the Venom fighter.

Even though the Condon Report, released to the public in 1969, lists this sighting as "unexplained" and admits that there probably was "at least one genuine UFO," no follow-up investigation was ever called for. The case was never publicized and ended up buried in the pages of Project Blue Book, the Air Force's official investigation into the UFO phenomenon.

The Condon Report concluded that further

study of UFOs was not worthwhile or justified, and the Air Force ended Project Blue Book, which had been in existence since 1952.

How many more cases like Bentwaters/Lakenheath are listed as "unexplained" by the Condon Report? How could the Condon Report state there was one genuine UFO at this sighting, then turn around and say further study of UFOs is not justified?

The late Dr. James MacDonald declared that "something in the nature of extraterrestrial devices engaged in something in the nature of surveillance lies at the heart of the UFO problem." MacDonald asked, "Doesn't a UFO case like Bentwaters/Lakenheath warrant more than a mere shrug of the shoulders from scientists?"

Shouldn't a genuine UFO sighting deserve further investigation? Apparently the Air Force didn't think so. What about you?

Deadly Collision

Millions of rocky objects circle the Sun between Mars and Jupiter in the area known as the asteroid belt. Many scientists believe these asteroids are what remains from the formation of the planets billions of years ago. The asteroids range in size from a few feet across to miles in diameter.

Picture this: A rock as huge as a city, traveling 100 times faster than a speeding bullet, comes hurtling out of the sky. Weighing more than a trillion tons, the giant asteroid is barely slowed by the Earth's atmosphere. In less than a second, mankind's worst nightmare strikes the ocean, raises the water temperature to

100,000 degrees, and instantly boils trillions of tons of seawater.

If this same asteroid crashed into the ground, its explosive force would be equal to 100 million megatons of TNT. The shock wave from the crash would destroy everything within 150 miles. Dirt, dust, and stone would shoot straight up into the atmosphere, blocking the sunlight. Buildings and trees would burst into flames, followed later by rain as sharp and biting as battery acid.

The impact of the asteroid would trigger an earthquake tens of thousands of times more powerful than the one in San Francisco in 1906. The quake would cause powerful sea waves, called tsunamis (pronounced "sue-nam-eez"), to rise several miles high and roll in toward the land at speeds of more than 400 miles per hour. Nine hundred miles away, the wall of water would still be about 1,500 feet high!

Death and destruction would be widespread. Agriculture would be impossible due to a thick dust cloud that would totally envelop the Earth. There would be no sunlight for more than six months, resulting in the collapse of the food chain.

The Earth would grow cold, plunging to subfreezing temperature. Whatever life-forms eventually survived this ordeal would be very different from the ones that lived on Earth before the deadly collision.

Sounds pretty awful, doesn't it? According to astronomer Donald Yeomans of the Jet Propulsion Laboratory in Pasadena, California, "Earth runs its course about the Sun in a swarm of asteroids. Sooner or later, our planet will be struck by one of them."

In fact, scientists say the Earth has been hit by meteorites at least 139 times—and they've found the giant craters to prove it, ("meteorite" is the term used to describe any object that passes through the Earth's atmosphere and reaches the ground). Many believe that a major hit 65 million years ago killed all the dinosaurs and most of the life on Earth at that time.

Small meteorites fall to Earth frequently with little or no injuries or destruction. What are the chances that a massive asteroid like the one described will collide with the Earth?

NASA (National Aeronautics and Space Administration) estimates that there are thousands of asteroids that cross Earth's orbit and are larger than half a mile in diameter. Because they can identify only a small number of them, NASA proposes a special early-warning system using powerful telescopes to look for large asteroids and other potential hazards from space.

The real danger lies in the size of the object. A meteorite which is larger than 30 feet across when it hits the Earth could cause death and destruction on a small scale and even trigger earthquakes.

According to astrophysicist Jack Hills of Los Alamos National Laboratory, it's estimated that objects larger than 300 feet hit the Earth every 5,000 years. Objects a half mile in diameter hit every 300,000 years. Whereas the really big ones, larger than 3 miles across, hit Earth every 10 to 30 million years.

So it's not likely an asteroid will hit Earth in the near future—or is it? *Newsweek* magazine stated that on March 23, 1989, an asteroid a half mile wide missed Earth by only 700,000 miles. That may sound like a lot, but if it had arrived just six hours later, it would have scored a direct hit on the Earth!

Another near miss occurred in January 1991, when an asteroid passed within about 110,000 miles of Earth. It was only about 30 feet in diameter so it would likely break apart and burn up in the atmosphere, too high to cause much damage.

The early-warning system proposed by NASA could detect large asteroids several weeks in advance of a collision with Earth. NASA scientists agree that the only way to defend against such a catastrophe would be to launch a rocket at the intruder armed with one or more nuclear-tipped missiles. Can such a rocket intercept a speeding asteroid? Would the missiles be able to explode on its surface? If both answers are yes, the resulting blast would push the asteroid far enough off course so that a collision with the Earth would be avoided. But can it be done? Scientists think so.

Newsweek declared that during a human lifetime there's a 1-in-10,000 chance that Earth will suffer a direct hit big enough to affect the future of mankind. The question is, will mankind be ready for it?

Climate Catastrophes

The great cities of America have been reduced to rubble by the advance of mile-thick sheets of ice and glaciers. Boston, New York, Philadelphia, and Chicago are uninhabitable frozen wastelands. As the glaciers advance in this new ice age, the sea level drops and land on the continental shelves is exposed.

Both human and animal life move southward. New cities and population centers are constructed in areas that once were deserts. Rain now falls on previously dry and barren regions, turning them into fertile grasslands.

But there is overcrowding and difficulty in relocating vast numbers of people who have become refugees in their own land. What was once the country's agricultural heartland is now a subarctic plain. Problems multiply as the government attempts to feed, clothe, and house these newly homeless, forced out by the harsh and persistent ice.

In southern areas, construction jobs are plentiful as new cities emerge on land that once was underwater. Americans adjust slowly as the capitol is moved to Dallas and that section of the city is renamed New Washington. Construction of a new White House is well under way and groups have formed to investigate the possibility of salvaging the Washington Monument and the Lincoln and Jefferson Memorials before the cold and ice destroy them completely.

Is this a scene from a new science-fiction movie, or could something like this really happen? The answers are no, it's not a movie, and yes, it could happen. In fact, some scientists believe the next ice age will begin within 2,000 years. That seems like a long time from now, considering the average life span of Americans is about 72 years. But in Earth's timeline, it's barely a blink of an eye.

Many scientists believe that the Earth's ice ages were connected with variations in its orbital cycles and axial tilt. Others believe climate swings were caused by the creation of the Himalayan mountain range 40 million years ago. The Himalayans obstructed wind movement, causing variations in the Earth's temperature.

Some scientists believe that the burning of fossil fuels and rain forests add more carbon dioxide into the atmosphere. This causes a rise in the Earth's surface temperatures and results in an artificial global warming, which may bring on another ice age sooner than expected.

How could warming, and not cooling, bring about the next ice age, you ask? The increase in temperature may warm the northern areas just enough for heavy snowfall to begin, but not so much that it melts off in the summer. The result is that the glaciers would grow, with the larger ice sheets reflecting more solar warmth back into space instead of absorbing it.

If the Earth's temperature rises even more markedly, the polar ice caps may begin to melt. When you consider the fact that there are 9 million cubic miles of ice on Earth, all that melted ice would make the sea level rise by about 200 feet. Water would eventually cover much of the low-lying borders of all the continents.

But don't panic! These are extreme case possibilities. Such changes would likely take place gradually over thousands of years or longer. As the glaciers traveled southward, people would slowly relocate to warmer areas. If the sea level slowly rose, inhabitants of coastal cities would move to higher ground. However, if these changes took place more rapidly, over dozens of years instead of thousands, it could prove quite disastrous for the people of the world.

Scientist and author Isaac Asimov, in his book *A Choice of Catastrophes*, suggests that advanced technology may keep the Earth's temperature in a safe range. According to Asimov, mirrors could be placed in space to reflect sunlight that would have missed the planet onto the Earth's surface. This would warm the temperature slightly if another ice age threatened. These same mirrors could reflect sunlight away from the Earth's surface to cool it slightly if ice cap melting was a danger.

As mankind continues to tamper with the Earth's atmosphere and the planet itself, it is uncertain how the world's climate will be affected. No one is absolutely sure what could trigger another ice age or melt the polar ice caps. Perhaps methods may eventually be developed for controlling the carbon dioxide content of the atmosphere. One thing is certain, however. Scientists are working hard to unlock the Earth's secrets and avoid possible catastrophes in the future.

Incidents in New Mexico

Dan Wilmot and his wife were relaxing on their front porch in Roswell, New Mexico, on the evening of July 2, 1947. It had been a hot summer day, and the Wilmots were enjoying the cool evening breeze.

"All of a sudden," said Dan, "a big glowing object zoomed out of the sky from the southeast. It was going northwest at a high rate of speed." The Wilmots watched in amazement as the oval-shaped object flew over their house and then out of sight.

A short time later, 75 miles southwest of Roswell, a rancher named Mac Brazel heard a strange explosion during a sudden and severe lightning storm. The next morning, he came

across wreckage scattered over a quarter-mile patch of land. It looked unusual, but Brazel didn't report his discovery to the sheriff until several days later when he finally went into town. The Air Force was quickly notified, and they took over the investigation and carried away the wreckage.

Since there had been an unusually high number of sightings in New Mexico and Arizona that summer, rumors about UFOs started flying. This area of the United States was also the site of top secret research involving atomic energy and development as well as rocket and missile experiments. Did alien spacecraft regularly monitor these areas of high scientific activity? Some people thought so.

On July 8, 1947, the public information officer at the Roswell Army Air Base issued a press release that was carried by newspapers and wire services throughout the world. It read:

The many rumors regarding the flying disc became a reality yesterday when the intelligence office of the 509th Bomb Group of the Eighth Air Force was fortunate enough to gain possession of a disc through the cooperation of one of the local ranchers and the sheriff's office of Chaves County.

Almost immediately an order stopping news releases came down over Roswell. Then, several hours later, the military announced that the object was a crashed weather balloon that had been mistaken for a flying disk. Later, torn-up pieces of an actual weather balloon were shown as evidence. Was the press release a mistake? Was the balloon wreckage substituted for the real wreckage of the spacecraft in an effort to calm the public and keep the incident a secret? Charles Berlitz and William Moore think so.

In their book, *The Roswell Incident*, Berlitz and Moore quote dozens of people who saw and described the real wreckage years later in interviews. "I didn't know what it was," said Major Jesse Marcel, staff officer in charge of intelligence at the Roswell Army Air Base in 1947, "but it most certainly wasn't any weather balloon."

Marcel went on to describe strange hieroglyphics and symbols on something that looked like balsa wood but was very hard. He mentioned pieces of a metal that looked like tinfoil but wasn't. It would not bend and could not be dented even with a 16-pound sledgehammer. According to Marcel, all the debris was loaded onto a B-29 airplane and flown to Wright-Patterson Field in Ohio. Three months later, Marcel was transferred to Washington, D.C.

Interviews with Bill and Bessie Brazel, Mac Brazel's children, and Floyd Proctor, Brazel's neighbor, all confirmed the strange lightweight but strong metal and the unusual hieroglyphics on parts of the wreckage.

According to Berlitz and Moore, the debris on the Brazel ranch was the result of an explosion on board the craft after it was struck by lightning during the electrical storm on the night of July 2. However, the main body of the spacecraft managed to fly 125 miles more before crashing to Earth near Socorro, New Mexico. Many years later, a number of witnesses claimed they had seen the actual disk itself back in 1947, as well as the dead bodies of several extraterrestrials on board, at this site near Socorro. These bodies were described by witnesses as three to four feet high, with large heads, oddly set eyes, no hair, and long arms.

Berlitz and Moore believe the Roswell and Socorro incidents were intentionally covered up by the military in the interest of national security. They believe the military was afraid to make the incidents public, fearing that other nations would duplicate the disks and be in a position to control the Earth. Furthermore, the authors claim that there are special top secret areas on certain Air Force bases today where the remains of spacecraft and actual aliens are kept and analyzed in an effort to uncover their secrets.

Jacques Vallee, in his book, *Revelations*, believes something did fall from the sky in 1947 and that the story was covered up by the Air Force. According to Vallee, it was not a weather balloon, but it wasn't a flying saucer, either. Since Roswell was the site of the first air base equipped with atomic bombs, Vallee theorizes that some top secret atomic device crashed during the electrical storm. Then the Air Force invented the weather balloon story, and even the flying saucer crash, in an effort to divert attention from this secret project.

Was it a weather balloon that crashed in New Mexico nearly fifty years ago? Was it an actual spacecraft, and were there really aliens on board? Or was it all a story to keep the public's attention away from our atomic secrets? Are UFOs and their alien pilots being kept secretly somewhere for research and study even today?

Berlitz and Moore comment on the appearance of the aliens according to witnesses, noting that "the features of head enlargement, hairlessness, elongation of arms and loss of height might be said to be a guess of how *we* will look in the far future." Considering current scientific theories about time travel, could these aliens, if they existed, have come from our own future?

There are so many questions and so few answers. It's uncertain whether the truth will ever be known.

Meanwhile, the mystery continues.

Tunnels of Blackness

Imagine traveling in deep space in the far future, trillions of miles from the Earth. "We're now approaching the constellation Cygnus, the Swan," announces the captain of the spaceship *Explorer*. Our mission is to investigate and confirm the existence of the black hole Cygnus X-1."

Looking out the porthole of the spacecraft, crew members see a small black dot surrounded by background stars. As *Explorer* approaches the black hole, the dot grows larger, filling up more of the sky. The hole itself is blacker than black, since it totally blocks off light from the other bodies around it. The nearby stars appear to form swirling rings around the hole.

"The gravitational field of the black hole is pulling us in," screams the captain suddenly. "I'm losing control. We're being sucked down!"

Hurtling through space, the ship now seems almost totally surrounded by blackness. The bright rings of stars appear to be behind *Explorer*. Instantly they are gone and there is complete darkness. No one on board will ever see the universe as they know it again.

At this stage in our scientific knowledge, there is no way that the crew and their spaceship could ever survive a trip through a black hole. First, the extreme gravitational forces would pull both the spaceship and its crew members apart. Second, the radiation levels are so high that survival would be impossible. Third, the tunnel within the black hole is one-way only. Once inside, there's no turning back and no escape. The spaceship would not be capable of exceeding the speed of light necessary to overcome the powerful gravitational pull. In addition, the tunnel is so unstable that any disturbance would cause it to close up.

If somehow all these problems could be overcome, and the *Explorer* was to make it through the black hole, where would the ship and crew end up? Scientists believe these black hole tunnels may be like time machines.

The *Explorer* could travel through the black hole and enter into a distant place in the universe sometime in the past or the future.

What are these black holes and how do scientists know so much about them? The theory states that giant stars eventually run out of energy, collapse inward, and explode as a supernova. The core of matter left behind by the explosion is so densely packed, and so strong in its gravitational pull, that nothing, not even light, can escape from it. A black hole formed from the matter left behind by the supernova explosion is called a stellar black hole.

Mini black holes were thought to have formed after the beginning of the universe 15 to 20 billion years ago. Their circular surface area (called the event horizon) could be less than an inch across. Yet the power of these tiny black holes would be equal to the power of a stellar black hole whose event horizon stretches over miles of space.

There are also supermassive black holes, believed to be located in the centers of galaxies. The diameter of their event horizons could stretch over hundreds of thousands of miles. In fact, scientists believe this type of black hole, as massive as millions of suns, is located in the center of our own Milky Way galaxy.

Since even light can't pass through black holes, they are invisible. So how do we know

they're there? Black holes give off radiation that can be detected in space by satellites. This helps scientists pinpoint the location of black holes throughout the universe.

At the center of every black hole is something called a singularity. This is a point where the density is so great that the usual laws of physics don't apply in regard to time and space.

Is the singularity a link to time travel or a connection to distant spots in the universe? Are black holes real or just scientific theory? Scientists are fairly certain of their existence, but will there ever be real proof?

No one knows for sure. These are just several of the incredible mysteries of space and the universe waiting to be solved.

Planet X

How much do we know about our own solar system? Not as much as scientists would like. There are many mysteries that still remain unsolved within this system we call home.

Mercury, Venus, Mars, Jupiter, and Saturn are all visible in the night sky without a telescope. They were recognized as planets by the ancient Sumerians as early as 3,000 B.C. Then thousands of years passed. It wasn't until 1781 that an English astronomer, Sir William Herschel, discovered the seventh planet in the solar system and named it Uranus.

Astronomers tracked Uranus for years in the nineteenth century and found discrepancies in its orbit. At times, it wasn't where it was supposed to be. It didn't appear to move in a regular pattern like the other planets. Why was Uranus off course? Astronomers believed an undiscovered planet was the cause of the disturbance.

The discovery of the planet Neptune in 1846 was credited to John Couch Adams, an Englishman, and Urbain LeVerrier of France. Yet many scientists felt that Neptune was not responsible for the irregular movements of Uranus. In fact, disturbances in Neptune's own orbit were discovered as well. Some declared there was an unknown planet still hidden in the outer solar system beyond Neptune.

An American named Percival Lowell searched unsuccessfully for this unknown body, which he called Planet X, from 1910 until his death in 1916. Lowell's calculations predicted that Planet X would have a mass seven times larger than the Earth's in order to have caused the disturbances in the orbits of Uranus and Neptune.

Years passed, and in 1930, an American named Clyde Tombaugh continued the search for Planet X. What he found instead was the ninth planet in the solar system, Pluto. Much smaller than Earth, Pluto couldn't have caused the disturbances. "It isn't massive enough," declared several scientists. "It could not be Lowell's Planet X!"

It wasn't until 1978 that James W. Christy

of the U.S. Naval Observatory discovered that Pluto had a satellite and named it Charon. Most of what scientists know today about the outer planets is credited to the numerous, detailed photographs taken by the *Voyager 2* spacecraft in the 1980s.

Pluto, Charon, and a satellite of Neptune called Triton, consist mainly of rocky material. This is unlike the other outer planets and their satellites, which are all made up mainly of gas and ice. Were Pluto, Charon, and Triton the result of a collision between Planet X and another satellite billions of years ago? Did Planet X cause the unusual movement in the orbits of Uranus and Neptune in the nineteenth century?

If Planet X does exist, it may have moved outward in a highly unusual orbit around the sun. This mysterious planet may not return to the same part of the solar system again for hundreds of years. This means that it would be almost impossible to discover its existence until that time. Even the Pioneer and Voyager spacecrafts have an unlikely chance of coming upon Planet X in the vastness of space.

Is Planet X the tenth planet of our solar system? Scientists don't know for sure, but the possibility definitely exists. In the meantime, they continue to search the skies.

Mysterious Circles

A pilot flying at a low altitude over wheat fields in southern England suddenly looked down and made a startling discovery. Much to his amazement, he saw five large and perfect circles in which the wheat had been mysteriously flattened in a strange, swirling pattern.

Once on the ground, he contacted the farmer who owned the fields and asked to examine them closer. "They weren't there yesterday," explained the astonished farmer.

The largest circle measured more than 40 feet across. The four smaller circles, each located at equally distant points outside the larger circle, measured more than 20 feet across.

Within the circles, the wheat stems were bent and flattened, but not broken or damaged in any way. In fact, they continued to grow horizontally and ripen. When the pilot tried to bend one of the nearby stems into the same position, it snapped off in his hands!

What powerful force could have flattened the crops in this particular swirling pattern, yet not have damaged them in any way? What did the circles mean? How were they created and by whom? There are many questions, but few answers.

Crop circles are not particularly unique in southern England. They've been appearing for decades in farmers' fields, but it wasn't until the 1980s that they were photographed and documented by Pat Delgado and Colin Andrews in their book, *Circular Evidence*.

Delgado and Andrews have discovered fields containing one to five circles. Some flattened circles are surrounded by rings of standing crops that, in turn, are surrounded by flattened rings.

In addition to the strange patterns of the circles, Delgado and Andrews have discovered that most seem to be created at night and a large number are near ponds, reservoirs, or underground water tanks.

Mysterious events also seem to be connected

with circle appearances. Numerous UFO sightings have occurred near circles, as well as reports of flashing lights and crackling noises. In
one case, the pilot of a Harrier jet ejected over
the exact spot where four circles were located.
The plane ditched pilotless into the Atlantic
hundreds of miles away. The pilot's body was
later found in a field overlooking the circles.
Officials had no idea why the pilot ejected from
the plane, since there had been no problem
with his aircraft.

Many believe this "flattened swirled crops
phenomenon," the term Delgado and Andrews use, is nothing more than a hoax created by practical jokers. "Faked circles are
obvious," say Delgado and Andrews, "compared to the precision, detail, and beauty of
the real ones."

In a demonstration of how a fake circle was
created, a person stood holding one end of a
rope while two others held on to the other end.
The two then trampled the crops down with
their boots to create the border of the circle.
Then they flattened the rest of the crops
within the border. The result was a circle, but
all the crops were damaged and broken, and
there was no swirled pattern.

In another attempt, two young men lay on
the ground and rolled over and over, directed
by two others who stood in the center. The re-

sult was more of a diamond shape than a circle, with damaged crops and no specific swirl pattern.

In a televised demonstration, a line of men holding a rope walked around a man who stood in one place holding one end of the rope. They formed a flattened circle but the crops were badly damaged.

Many have tried to duplicate the circles, but it is impossible to do so without damaging the crops. The real circle patterns are too complicated to duplicate correctly.

There are never any entry or exit paths to and from the circles in the fields. Even if only one or two people walk through a wheat field, a path is always visible. Therefore, whatever force is responsible for creating these circles must come from above the field. The untouched crops surrounding the circles suggest no ground contact at all.

Are these mysterious circles and rings the result of UFOs? Delgado and Andrews give examples of circles appearing all over the world, not just in the English countryside. Have circular-shaped spacecraft, controlled by an unknown intelligence, been visiting Earth for years? If so, why these particular areas, and what do they hope to accomplish?

If the circles were not caused by UFOs,

what powerful force exists in the universe that could create such a strange phenomenon?

In either case, further scientific investigation is needed. Perhaps additional research will discover the answer to what remains an unsolved mystery.

Halley's and Other Comets

For many years, comets were looked upon as signs of disaster and death. Whenever they appeared, terrible things happened and comets took the blame. They've been linked to the destruction of Jerusalem (A.D 66), the death of Julius Caesar (44 B.C.), the black plague (530 B.C.), and the eruption of Mount Vesuvius (684 B.C.), among other things.

Although astronomers watched, studied, and recorded the position of comets in the sky, it was the Englishman Edmund Halley (rhymes with "valley") who attempted to calculate the exact orbit of one he observed in 1682. In the course of his research, Halley discovered that the comets of 1531, 1607, and 1682 were not different, but were one and the same! He predicted that it would return again in the year 1758. Unfortunately, he died in 1742 and never lived to see the return of his comet. But he was proven correct and the comet was named after him.

Halley's comet came back in 1835 and then again in 1910. Astronomers predicted the Earth would pass through the tail, and many people were convinced that the end of the world was at hand. Some actually committed suicide, while others waited to be killed by the so-called poisonous gases in the comet's tail. Of course, nothing happened.

One woman remembers seeing it as a child in 1910 and described Halley's comet as a "small sun with a tail." It returned again in December 1985, and is due back in July of 2061 and then again in March of 2134. Don't forget to mark your calendar!

What are comets, anyway? They're believed to be the remains of matter from which the solar system was formed. According to astronomer Fred Whipple, comets are "dirty snowballs," balls of icy substances such as water, ammonia, and methane mixed in with dust and small bits of rocky materials. The center or core of the comet is usually solid rock. Space probes in 1986 revealed Halley's core to be about the size of Manhattan Island, New York (about 13 miles long and 2.25 miles wide).

These balls of ice and rock remain frozen in the far reaches of the solar system. Billions of comets circle the Sun in the Kuiper belt, just past Uranus and extending beyond Neptune. The huge Oort cloud beyond Pluto is also home to billions more.

As a comet approaches the Sun, the warmth causes its temperature to rise. Some of the ice melts, releasing dust particles. Reflected sunlight makes the head of the comet appear very bright, surrounded by a haze of dust. Many comets have a very long tail, which consists of dust and gas pushed away from the Sun by an invisible solar wind of high-speed particles.

As the comet circles the Sun and heads back to the depths of the solar system, it starts to cool, the tail disappears, and the comet once again becomes a frozen ball of ice. With each passage of the Sun some of the comet's material is lost. Eventually, many fade away, leaving behind the rocky core of a thin layer of dust particles.

Every once in a while, a comet's orbit changes, due to the gravitational pull of a nearby star or planet, or even a collision between two comets. This causes them to either leave the solar system altogether or fall in toward the Sun and inner planets. As the Sun warms the comet, its surface erupts with jets of gas and dust, which may slightly shift the path of the comet even further.

According to *Newsweek* magazine, "about 200 comets revisit Earth's environs more often than once every two centuries . . . But no one knows how many never-before-seen comets are heading our way."

In October of 1992, astronomer Brian Marsden declared that Comet Swift-Tuttle, observed in 1862 and again in 1992, has a 1-in-10,000 chance of hitting Earth on its next pass in 2126. Could Swift-Tuttle's jets push it into a collision course with Earth? Marsden says it's possible, though other scientists say "there is no evidence of a threat from Swift-Tuttle."

Should we breathe a sigh of relief or start to worry? Astronomer Clark Chapman declared in *Newsweek*: "For those [comets] coming in from the far reaches of the solar system [for the first time], we have virtually no chance of seeing them until they get close."

As with asteroids, the first line of defense against a comet on a collision course with Earth is to launch a rocket armed with nuclear-tipped missiles. If the missile makes a direct hit, the comet could explode into millions of pieces that could still hit Earth. The key is to explode the nuclear-tipped missile

near the comet to melt the frozen gases. It is hoped that the resulting jets of gas and dust would steer the comet from its deadly path.

It's still a long shot that Earth will take a major hit from a comet in the next few hundred years, but the possibility does exist. In the meantime, astronomers continue to search the skies and learn as much as they can about these mysterious and sometimes threatening objects.

Through Space
and Time

The year is 2294. The Brooks family is planning their summer vacation.

"Well, kids, I've got six weeks off and we've got a choice of two exciting trips," explains Dad. "We can visit several of the vacation-theme planets in the Andromeda galaxy, or we can do what your mother wants and travel back in time to colonial Pennsylvania."

"Let's spend our first three weeks basking on the green sands and red seas of the newest colonized vacation planet in the Andromeda galaxy," says Mom. "Then we'll spend our last three weeks in eighteenth-century Philadelphia, reliving our nation's history. Bring out the powdered wigs and hoop skirts!"

Sounds impossible, doesn't it? Traveling back in time or to distant parts of the universe is pure science fiction. But there are scientists today who believe it may someday be science fact!

What could make it all possible are wormholes. In theory, wormholes are thought by scientists to be like subway tunnels to distant parts of the universe and to the past and future. Some are associated with the singularity at the center of black holes. Here the density is so great that time and space turn in on themselves and form a wormhole.

But scientists believe there may be many difficulties in traveling through wormholes. They are very unstable and tend to close off, resulting in crushed spaceships and crews. Travelers would also be subjected to severe stretching forces as well as high radiation levels.

It is believed that these problems could be overcome in wormholes *not* connected to black holes. Scientists would simply apply exotic matter (which has negative energy density) to the wormhole to keep it from closing. The wormholes would also be designed to minimize stretching forces and radiation.

According to Barry Parker in his book *Cosmic Time Travel*, to make the wormhole into a time tunnel: "All you need to do is move one end of the wormhole at high speed (close to the speed of light) or place it in a strong gravitational field . . . Once this is done, you could go in one end and come out the other at an earlier time. Or . . . gō in the other end, go through it in the opposite direction, and come out in the future."

It's not certain that wormholes even exist, or that exotic matter could ever be produced. Right now they're scientific theory. But let's assume they can and go on to the problem of causality. This means that the effect of something always comes after its cause.

What would happen if causality is violated? For example, if a person travels back in time and somehow manages to stop the marriage of his or her grandparents, what would happen to that person? How could he or she come to exist if his or her grandparents never married each other and never gave birth to his or her parents?

Here's another example. A women travels back in time a few weeks and sees herself. There would be two of the same people. Could they have a conversation with each other? Traveling into the past may result in these very strange types of situations that would violate causality.

Will wormholes someday be used as a subway system to the far reaches of the universe?

Could such a network of wormholes be in use even now by an extremely advanced civilization in a far-off galaxy? What about time travel into the past or future?

It sounds possible in principle, but Parker declares it could be hundreds or even thousands of years before it is realized.

Remember that all new theories sound crazy at first. The Earth is round, not flat? Ridiculous! Fly across the ocean like a bird in a huge ship with wings? Preposterous! Land men on the Moon? It'll never happen! What started out as theories eventually became facts. Traveling to distant places in the universe, and back or forward in time, may someday become a reality, too.

"There appears to be nothing in physics that prevents time travel," declares Parker. "But achieving it is something else." And that's where the challenge lies.

Cover-up in Texas

"Did you see a flash of light in that field?" asked farmhand Pedro Saucedo. He and his friend, Joe Salaz, were driving along Route 116 four miles west of the small town of Levelland, Texas. It was the night of November 2, 1957.

As both men looked off to the field on their right, they suddenly saw a bright yellow-white light. The strange object rose into the air and passed over the truck. There was "a great sound and rush of wind," said Saucedo. "It sounded like thunder, and the truck rocked from the blast."

Saucedo felt a wave of heat as the torpedo-shaped object passed over the truck and the truck's engine and headlights suddenly shut off. Once the object (described as about 200 feet long and moving very fast) sped away into the distance, the truck's headlights came back on and the engine started up again. Saucedo reported the incident to Officer A. J. Fowler of the Levelland Police Department.

Fowler didn't give the sighting much thought until about an hour later when a man named Jim Wheeler called in a similar story. He was driving on Route 116 a few miles east of Levelland when he saw a 200-foot glowing egg-shaped object in the middle of the road. Wheeler's lights and engine died. When the object took off into the sky, his headlights came back on and he was able to restart the engine.

Next, Jose Alvarez called in to report a similar sighting, but this time it happened on Route 51 about 11 miles north of town. After midnight, another sighting was reported by a student named Newell Wright on Route 116. He had car trouble and saw an oval-shaped object about 125 feet in size and giving off a blue-green light. When the craft rose straight up and sped off, Wright's car began working normally again.

At 12:15 A.M. Frank Williams saw the UFO and also experienced car trouble. He said the light from the object was going on and off before the craft sped off with a thunderous noise.

After five calls, Officer Fowler knew some-

thing unusual was flying in the skies over
Levelland, so he called Sheriff Weir Clem and
informed him of the night's events. Sheriff
Clem .lecided he wanted to see this strange object himself and drove to the area.

The next sighting was at 12:45 A.M. on
Route 116. Ronald Martin's truck died and
then he saw "a big ball of fire drop on the highway." It changed colors, took off, and his truck
ran normally again.

The seventh sighting was reported by another trucker, named James Long, at 1:15 A.M.
The eighth sighting was by Sheriff Clem and
Deputy Pat McCulloch about five miles outside
of town. They described "an oval-shaped light
looking like a brilliant red sunset across the
highway."

Nearly all the witnesses had engine and
headlight failure. They all described an oval-
shaped object 125 to 200 feet long, and they all
saw bright colors of light. Several heard thunderous noises as the craft took off.

Several days later, an Air Force investigator
who spent a day in the area concluded that the
Levelland sightings were caused by ball lightning, not by a UFO. The Air Force report
claimed there had been an electrical storm in
the area at the time. Although it had been
overcast and damp, there was no lightning or
electrical storm reported that night.

Ball lightning is an electrical discharge, usually accompanied by thunder, that may appear as a brilliant ball instead of the familiar jagged streaks or flashes in the sky. However, ball lightning doesn't cause engines to die or headlights to go out. Nor does ball lightning land on highways or fields and then take off at high speeds. Finally, ball lightning has never been known to reach a size of 125 to 200 feet across. The Air Force's explanation does not appear to explain satisfactorily what eyewitnesses reported seeing.

What really happened that night in Levelland, Texas, in 1957? More than half a dozen people, completely independent of each other, saw and experienced similar and unusual things. Did they all imagine the same incident? It's not likely.

Apparently, all these witnesses saw a mysterious flying object that could not be correctly identified. Was it a spacecraft piloted by extraterrestrials or a secret military project piloted by human beings? Was it really ball lightning or the result of overactive imaginations? Did the Air Force cover up the incident as quickly as possible, and if so, why?

The answers will never be known, and the sightings at Levelland remain a mystery.

Is Anybody Out There?

Many scientists have compared the search for extraterrestrial intelligence in the universe to finding "a needle in the cosmic haystack." So how do we determine who's out there?

Radio astronomer Frank Drake developed a way of estimating the number of intelligent civilizations in the Milky Way galaxy that are able to transmit and receive radio signals. It's assumed that such signals are the most likely way that planets will communicate with each other.

This formula, called the Drake Equation, takes into account many factors, including the average number of stars formed each year, the stars with planets, planets with environments that can support life, and those that actually do support life.

Only a small fraction of planets that support life will have intelligent life, and only a small portion of that intelligent life will develop radio or even choose to contact others in the universe.

A very important factor in the Drake Equation is the life span of a civilization. How long will the civilization last after developing radio communication, considering the risk of nuclear war and other catastrophes?

Thomas McDonough, in his book *The Search for Extraterrestrial Intelligence*, uses the Drake Equation to estimate the number of advanced civilizations in our own galaxy. Considering there are about 400 billion stars in the Milky Way and most have planets, he estimates there are about 40 billion Earth-type planets.

About one in ten, or 4 billion, may develop some type of life, but how many will develop intelligent life? McDonough estimates one in a hundred, or 40 million, civilizations will develop intelligent life. Since astronomers have proved that the laws of physics are the same throughout the universe, he believes about one in every ten civilizations with intelligent life, or 4 million civilizations, will develop radio communication.

Have some of these civilizations already destroyed themselves with nuclear weapons or been destroyed by collisions with comets or asteroids? McDonough concludes that only one-thousandth of the 4 million civilizations are still in existence right now. That's at least 4,000 worlds waiting to be contacted by Earth!

Isaac Asimov, in his book *Extraterrestrial Civilizations*, estimates there are 530,000 planets in our galaxy on which a technological civilization like Earth's is now in existence. A 1961 conference on extraterrestrial life came up with a figure of 100 to 100 million civilizations.

However, there are some scientists who believe only Earth is capable of communicating with other worlds. Physicist Frank Tipler states: "If a civilization approximately at our level had ever existed in the galaxy, their spaceships would already be here." He concludes, "Since they are not here, they do not exist."

A radio message traveling at the speed of light would take 100,000 years to travel from one end of the Milky Way galaxy to the other. If intelligent civilizations were only hundreds of light-years from each other, it would still take centuries for messages to be sent and received.

At this moment, the first radio signal broadcast to space in 1974 from Puerto Rico is still traveling outward across the galaxy and is now about 20 light-years away from Earth. That message may make contact with another civilization 50 years from now, or 150 years from now, or never.

It is possible that radio messages are traveling to Earth right now from other parts of the galaxy. But it could take several lifetimes before we intercept them. It all depends on the life span of the civilization sending the messages. The older the world, the farther and longer the signals have been traveling.

There are other possible explanations as to why there is what David Brin, in the book *First Contact*, calls "the great silence." Perhaps there are fewer Earth-like planets than astronomers think, or maybe some advanced civilizations do not want to make contact with or explore other areas of the universe. Could extraterrestrials believe Earth people are too dangerous and primitive to contact? Then there's the possibility that aliens may already be in contact with some people on Earth.

If contact is someday made with intelligent life on another world, what would these aliens look like? Most scientists seem to agree that the special ingredients that make up the recipe for life on the planet Earth would not likely be duplicated.

According to scientist Carl Sagan: "The only thing that's guaranteed is that life elsewhere will not be like life here. . . . It would be astonishing if anybody who looked very much like you or me arose elsewhere."

Science fiction writer Ray Bradbury agrees. "Nothing on Earth will be duplicated on any other planet . . . all the things that fly in the air will be different, all the things in the sea will be different, and all the things on the land will be different."

Just as past explorers set out in search of new worlds and the opportunities that came with them, Earth's scientists are prepared to unravel the mysteries of extraterrestrial intelligence in the universe.

Messages to
the Unknown

Imagine a lonely sailor, the only survivor of a shipwreck at sea. He has managed to swim to a tiny deserted island in the middle of the vast Pacific Ocean. The sailor has salvaged some food, water, and supplies from the wreck.

Overwhelmed by what has happened to him, the man carefully writes out a message on a scrap of dry paper, giving his name and the last location of his vessel. He folds up the message and inserts it into an empty bottle he has saved from the ship.

Walking offshore as far as possible, the man throws the bottle into the water and the current takes it out into the vastness of the ocean. Before he falls asleep that night, the man hopes someone will eventually find his message, thousands of miles away, and rescue him. But in the back of his mind, he realizes the chances are very slim, and instead concentrates on staying alive from one day to the next.

This is exactly what astronomers have done, but on a much larger scale. Instead of the Pacific Ocean, the messages have been sent into the far reaches of outer space. Instead of hoping to be rescued, scientists are attempting to make contact with other intelligent forms of life.

Consider the mind-boggling size of the universe. There are 100 billion stars in our Milky Way galaxy alone, and billions of other galaxies exist. The chances of direct contact are probably no better than of someone's finding the sailor's message in the bottle and rescuing him. But the messages *are* being sent because such a contact would change mankind forever!

The very first message was carried by the *Pioneer 10* and *Pioneer 11* spacecraft launched in 1972 by NASA (National Aeronautics and Space Administration). *Pioneer 10* was the first space probe to fly by Jupiter, and in 1983 it became the first object to leave the solar system forever when it passed Neptune and Pluto.

The message itself was written on an aluminum plaque and mounted on sections of the spacecraft that protected it from dust and other space particles. One side of the message consisted of the naked figures of a man and a woman. The man's right hand was raised up as if to wave a friendly greeting. Both figures were standing in front of an outline of the spacecraft.

The other side of the plaque showed the Milky Way galaxy and the position of our Sun within it. There were small pictures of the planets in the solar system, and basic math and chemistry symbols.

The first broadcasted message to space from the giant radio telescope in Arecibo, Puerto Rico, was sent in 1974. The message was beamed toward 300,000 stars in the constellation of Hercules, 25,000 light-years away. It noted the location of the Sun and planets, stating that this communication was from the third planet, Earth. Then it described what humans looked like and what their bodies were made of.

In a little less than 25,000 years, this message will finally arrive at its destination. But don't get too excited. If there *is* a reply, it will take another 25,000 years for the answer to come back!

In 1977, *Voyager 1* and *Voyager 2* were

launched by NASA. They were bigger and more advanced than the Pioneers, but their missions were similar—to fly by the outer planets (Jupiter, Saturn, Uranus, Neptune, and Pluto), take detailed photographs, then travel out of the solar system into other parts of the galaxy.

In 1993, the two Voyagers passed through the true edge of the solar system, called the heliopause. This is the place where solar winds, which are electrically charged particles from the Sun, meet similar particles from space, producing strong radio signals.

The two Voyagers carried a message consisting of a videodisk that included spoken words, music, and photographs. On the cover of the disk were pictures instructing how to use and play it. The disk itself contained scientific information and greetings from the Secretary-General of the United Nations and from Jimmy Carter, who was President of the United States at the time. There were also messages in different languages and music from all over the world and throughout history, from classical to rock and roll.

In addition to these scientifically planned messages to space, it's interesting to note that Earth has been broadcasting other messages to space in the form of television and even radio shows for decades. Imagine, some form of intelligent life in a galaxy light-years away may be watching "I Love Lucy" reruns. What would aliens think about Earth people after seeing the antics of Lucy, Ricky, Fred, and Ethel?

Red Glowing Disks

On the night of July 14, 1952, the skies above Norfolk, Virginia, were crystal clear with unlimited visibility. A Pan American DC-4 was making a routine flight from New York to Miami, Florida.

"Check out that reddish glow in the distance," said Second Officer William B. Nash in the cockpit.

"I see it," replied Copilot William Fortenberry. "It's just east of the city of Newport News."

"There are six bright lights now," stated Nash, "and they look like they're headed straight for us, and very fast."

"How fast could they be going?" asked Fortenberry as the glowing red objects streaked under the airliner. Suddenly, they made a sharp turn and reversed direction.

"Look, there are two more now—eight of them," said Nash, "and they're headed north of Newport News."

"They must have traveled at least fifty miles in twelve, say fifteen seconds," declared Fortenberry. "That's something like twelve thousand miles per hour!" The two men looked at each other in disbelief.

After landing in Miami and filing a report of the incident, the pilots were contacted the next day by Air Force intelligence officers. Nash described the objects as a formation of glowing red disks traveling at high speed. "Their shape was clearly outlined and circular," stated Nash. "The edges were well defined, not fuzzy. The exposed edges appeared to be about fifteen feet thick, and the top surface seemed flat." He added, "In shape and proportion, they were much like coins."

The Air Force investigators admitted to Nash that they had received seven other reports describing the formation of red disks traveling fast and making abrupt directional changes!

From their testimony, it's obvious that Nash and Fortenberry didn't just see random glowing lights in the sky. They clearly observed disks flying in specific patterns and changing directions. Were these disks piloted by intelligent beings?

In his 1963 book, *The World of Flying Saucers*, Donald Menzel dismisses the sightings by Nash and Fortenberry. He theorizes that the objects were the result of a combination of ground lights near the cities of Newport News and Norfolk, and clouds and humidity inversions in the air.

Menzel believes that a ground light could be seen as a series of glowing lights due to clouds or inversion layers of temperature or humidity. However, a Virginia weather report for the night of July 14 stated no temperature inversion, unlimited visibility, no haze, and at lower altitudes (the DC-4 was at 8,000 feet), the sky was cloudless and clear.

Nash and Fortenberry clearly stated they saw well-defined edges to the disks, not hazy or fuzzy edges. The two experienced pilots and veterans of World War II made specific observations. Surely they could tell the difference between a series of shimmering light images and eight disks flying in high-speed formation.

Did Nash and Fortenberry see unidentified flying objects that July night in 1952? It seems so. Were they spacecraft controlled by intelligent beings from another world? No one will ever know for sure what they were.

The official U.S. Air Force report concluded that these sightings were "unexplained."

Life on Mars—Past, Present, Future

People have always been fascinated by the planet Mars. Perhaps that's because of its many similarities to our own world. Mars has a 24.5-hour day, and there are polar ice caps that were visible even to eighteenth-century astronomers.

An Italian astronomer named Giovanni Schiaparelli made an interesting discovery about Mars in 1877. He noticed dark markings on the planet's surface that looked long and narrow. Schiaparelli believed they were bodies of water and called them *canali*, the Italian world for "channels." But it was translated by British and American scientists to mean "canals."

This mistake turns out to be very important. Channels are *natural* bodies of water, which is what Schiaparelli described. But canals are waterways constructed for a specific purpose by intelligent beings. Therefore, in people's minds, the canals on Mars were built by living and breathing Martians.

The idea of life on Mars became very popular, even taken for granted. An American astronomer named Percival Lowell was an influential supporter of an advanced Martian civilization. In one of his several books about Mars, Lowell explained that the Martians were a peaceful people who were trying to stop their planet from drying out and becoming a desert wasteland. Their network of surface canals was part of a giant irrigation project to save the planet and the Martian race.

In 1897, author H. G. Wells published *War of the Worlds*, a book in which Martians invade the Earth and attempt to take over the planet with advanced weapons. The invaders are defeated in the end by bacteria that are deadly to the Martians but harmless to Earth people.

The popularity of Wells's story changed the way people thought about extraterrestrials. Many began to believe that Martians and all aliens from space were threatening killers, not peace-loving civilized beings.

The possibility of life on Mars decreased in the twentieth century as scientists uncovered more information about the Martian climate and temperature.

Although Mars is often mild around the equator in the daytime, the night is as cold as Antarctica. Such a large drop in temperature means that the atmosphere is very thin and unable to absorb the daytime heat. This thin atmosphere could not protect the Martian surface and possible life-forms from the Sun's ultraviolet radiation like Earth's atmosphere does.

In 1947, astronomer Gerard Peter Kuiper detected carbon dioxide in Mars's atmosphere, but no oxygen or nitrogen. These factors indicated it was unlikely there was intelligent life, as we know it, on Mars. But had there been intelligent life in the past? Could there still be primitive life-forms on the planet? Could certain life-forms have adapted themselves to these harsh conditions?

The answers started coming in 1965. That was the year the Mariner space probe flew by Mars and returned twenty-two pictures to Earth. These photographs showed a barren world of large moonlike craters and no signs of life anywhere.

In 1969, *Mariner 6* and *Mariner 7* sent back pictures of volcanoes and lava plains from Mars. There was even evidence of water ice in the polar ice caps. Since water is essential to all living creatures, hopes were again raised about the possibility of life.

Photographs from *Mariner 9* in 1971 mapped out the details of the entire Martian surface. The southern hemisphere appeared to be a bleak, cratered, moonlike wasteland, while the northern hemisphere contained more interesting features. Mountain chains were discovered, and what looked like ancient river valleys and riverbeds. Did water flow here in the past? Could life really have existed?

The *Viking 1* and *Viking 2* spacecraft launched in 1975 landed on Mars in 1976 in two different areas. The areas were chosen for their landing safety and not for their interesting terrain. Both Vikings conducted experiments with the Martian soil, analysis of its content, and attempts to detect possible lifeforms or fossils. The Vikings also sent back color photographs of the Martian landscape that showed a light pink sky, the result of red dust in the atmosphere.

The results of the Viking experiments indicated the absence of organic compounds in the soil. It is assumed by scientists that if these compounds are not detected, life is not present.

The Viking experiments proved that in two particular spots on the surface of Mars, life didn't exist. There are many other more interesting areas to explore that might show evidence of Martian life or fossil remains. Although Mars is half the size of Earth, its land area is nearly the same, and no samples were taken by Viking below the surface of the planet.

The Viking biology team leader, Harold Klein, declared, "I believe that on the basis of the data we have in hand, we cannot conclusively say that there is life on Mars . . . and we cannot conclusively say that there is no life on Mars."

Many scientists believe that a few billion years ago Mars had rivers, seas, and oceans, as well as a dense atmosphere similar to that of ancient Earth. The thick carbon dioxide atmosphere retained heat, allowing running water to exist on the surface of the planet. Today, the atmospheric pressure is too low for liquid water. It would evaporate immediately and boil away.

What accounted for the disappearance of water on Mars's surface and for the less dense atmosphere? Apparently Mars lost the ability to recycle carbon dioxide back into the atmosphere and maintain a warming greenhouse effect. Thus, it couldn't trap heat energy from the Sun and slowly, over time, Mars froze.

Scientists believe the planet is in an ice age and the surface water and a large part of the atmosphere are frozen in the polar ice caps. Other water may exist deep underground. In fact, many feel that underground water resources can be reached by deep drilling.

Before the Martian ice age, primitive life might very well have existed in the oceans and seas on Mars. Perhaps some type of life-form gradually adjusted to the increasingly bleak conditions and some living organism has survived somewhere on the planet or even underground. Even a fossilized trace of past Martian life would be a great discovery.

Why is it so important to detect life on Mars, many ask. There are a number of answers. First, we on Earth would know we are not alone in the universe. Second, we'd gain a greater understanding of how life evolved on our planet, as well as on Mars. Third, if we were to discover some type of life-form, it would greatly increase the likelihood of life in distant worlds in faraway galaxies throughout the universe.

The next mission to Mars may consist of an

unmanned roving vehicle that could travel to different areas on the planet's surface and conduct various experiments. Future missions could include a manned flyby of the planet, manned landings, and a permanent base on Mars.

Eventually, colonies may thrive and grow near the base, and babies would be born. It is these children and their families who would become the Martians of the future!

Nemesis—The Death Star

A pattern has emerged in the Earth's history. Geologists have discovered that mass extinctions, called Great Dyings by Isaac Asimov in his book *Asimov's Guide to Halley's Comet*, seem to occur every 26 to 30 million years. The most well-known of these happened when the dinosaurs and two-thirds of all life on Earth were wiped out 65 million years ago.

Many scientists believe that a collision between Earth and an asteroid or comet caused the death of the dinosaurs. This theory was further supported by the fact that rock formations discovered from that time period showed high levels of iridium, a metal that is rare on Earth but common in meteorites.

If these theories are correct, and the mass extinctions by giant meteorites have occurred every 26 to 30 million years, one big question remains. What caused the meteorites to crash into Earth in the first place?

There is a theory suggested by several American scientists that an unknown object moves around our Sun in a distant and unusual orbit. They believe that the Sun has a sister star, an as-yet-undetected companion. (It's not unusual for stars to have a companion star.) This sister star—called Nemesis, or the death star—is named after the Greek goddess of doom.

Beyond Pluto, there is an area in space called the Oort cloud. Within this area are billions of comets in orbit around the Sun. Any disturbances in the Oort cloud would cause a great number of otherwise stable comets to fall in toward the Sun, where one or more might collide with Earth.

Suppose Nemesis takes 26 to 30 million years to make one complete orbit around the Sun. Its unusual orbit causes it to spend much of its time far away from the solar system and only a short time near the planets. The gravitational pull of such a star passing through the Oort cloud, even a small, dim star like Nemesis, would have a disastrous effect.

Thousands, perhaps millions, of comets,

knocked out of their orbits by Nemesis, would come speeding into the solar system. A few would be likely to crash into the Earth and a large hit could spell doom for mankind.

Is this what happened to the dinosaurs and in the mass extinctions since? The last Great Dying, a term coined by Isaac Asimov to describe such mass extinctions, was 11 million years ago. So the next one isn't expected for 15 million years or more. So far Nemesis has escaped detection by astronomers. Some say it's too dim and cold to be seen. Others say it's a Brown Dwarf, falling somewhere between a planet and a star.

If Nemesis does disturb the comets in the Oort cloud, what are the chances one will hit the earth? Frank Close, in his book, *Apocalypse When*, describes it this way: "If there are 100 billion comets in the Oort cloud, and if as few as one in one hundred is disturbed by a passing star, then one billion comets have entered the solar system. That makes it almost certain that a comet will hit us someday."

Is Nemesis the cause of this pattern of mass extinctions? It hasn't been proven that the death star even exists. But if it does, it should be able to be spotted by astronomers by the turn of the century. Then there will be millions of years to prepare a defense to save the Earth.

Film at 11

Skyhawk fighter-bombers of the Royal Air Force were put on alert after UFO sightings in New Zealand in late December 1978. It all started on the night of December 21, when the captain of a cargo plane on his way from the city of Blenheim to Christchurch reported seeing "a number of white lights."

Five unidentified objects were confirmed on radar by Wellington Air Traffic Control. A few hours later, a second sighting of unusual objects was reported and picked up on radar by Wellington.

"Something is coming toward us at a tremendous speed," declared Captain Vern Powell. "It was moving so fast it was leaving a tail behind it on the radar screen." Powell estimated the object traveled 15 miles in 5 seconds, which is about 10,800 miles per hour. There were no explanations for the sightings.

The following week, Australian television Channel O in Melbourne planned to do a story on the incident. Reporter Quentin Fogarty decided to fly the same route to reconstruct what took place for the television viewers. The flight was scheduled for the night of December 30.

Fogarty recorded his opening statement for the cameras on board the plane at 12:10 A.M. "We're exactly on the same route taken by Captain Powell when he encountered those mysterious objects. It's a beautiful clear night outside and naturally we'll be looking for anything unusual."

Suddenly, one of the pilots called Fogarty into the cockpit. The two men saw several bright globes of light and Wellington radar confirmed them. "Let's hope they're friendly," said Fogarty.

The night's adventures had begun. For nearly an hour the objects appeared and disappeared near the airplane, maneuvering underneath and from one side to the other, but all the while keeping a safe distance. TV cameraman David Crockett was able to shoot several thousand frames of 16-millimeter color movie film of the UFOs.

Crockett later described one as "a transparent sphere on top with a brightly lit saucer-shaped bottom." Never before in the history of UFO sightings had there been a radar, visual, and photographic sighting of a single incident. Once the television crew arrived back in Melbourne, the film was immediately sent to the United States for a detailed analysis.

Some officials claimed that the mysterious lights were probably the planet Venus or even meteor showers. But most of the scientists who studied the film agreed that they could not explain the objects, and they were not prepared to identify what they were.

It's obvious something unusual did take place that night in 1978 in the skies over New Zealand. The Royal Air Force decided not to take any chances, and their standby alert lasted for several days after the incident.

Primitive Life-forms

Most scientists agree that Earth is the only planet in our solar system on which intelligent life has evolved. But there are several possible worlds in our own backyard on which varieties of primitive life-forms may one day be discovered.

The environment of Antarctica on Earth is somewhat similar to Mars. Its extreme cold temperatures don't seem to bother the algae, fungi, bacteria, and insects that thrive there. That's why scientists are hopeful about finding microscopic life or fossilized remains on Mars.

Going to the other extreme, there are heat-loving bacteria, called thermophiles. These actually grow and thrive in the boiling waters of hot springs found in Yellowstone National Park. Some thermophiles can live and breed in very acidic hot water. Others are able to absorb and make use of sulfur compounds. Could similar bacteria survive on a planet such as Venus?

Surface temperatures reach 800 to 900 degrees Fahrenheit on Venus, and the Venusian cloud layer is made up of sulfuric acid drops. Until space probes can land on the surface, perform experiments, and take soil samples successfully, no one will really know. What is certain is that human beings and similar lifeforms could never endure the harsh conditions on Venus.

Can life exist under intense pressure? It can and does right here on Earth. Fish and shrimp live at ocean depths of up to 35,000 feet, where water pressure is eight tons per square inch. If these fish can adapt themselves to such pressurized conditions, could some type of primitive life-form adapt itself to the very dense, pressurized atmosphere of Jupiter?

The largest planet in our solar system, Jupiter consists mainly of gas and liquid. Dense clouds surround the planet above oceans of hydrogen, helium, ammonia, and methane, and continuous and huge whirling storms. The deeper one goes into the clouds and the closer to the surface, the more the pressure and temperature rise.

However, in the outer cloud layer, the temperature and pressure are similar to ancient Earth's. Could life exist in the upper clouds of Jupiter? Could there be creatures that float in the upper layers of the atmosphere and never sink into the deeper, more dangerous layers?

Some scientists believe such life-forms, if they do exist, might resemble hot-air balloons. Other creatures with wings might fly through the upper clouds, riding the currents of Jupiter's constant storms. At some time in the future, robotic space probes may be sent to uncover the secrets of this mysterious planet, which is 1,300 times the size of Earth.

Most life-forms require sunlight for energy. However, certain organisms on Earth have been found in the pitch-black natural hot water openings (called "hydrothermal vents") on the ocean floor. These organisms get their energy from minerals that leak out of the Earth's core. If life could develop under these conditions on Earth, perhaps organisms can exist on Jupiter's moon, Europa.

Scientists believe the surface of Europa is a sheet of water ice many miles thick. Beneath this icy crust is an ocean that may be as deep as 30 miles. This liquid ocean on Europa could contain all kinds of creatures that get their

food and energy from the bottom of the sea and not from sunlight. Europa definitely deserves exploration by the scientists of the future.

There are other places in our solar system on which primitive life-forms may now exist or might have developed in the past. Titan, the largest moon of Saturn, has a dense atmosphere that consists mainly of nitrogen. Scientists believe there may be liquids on Titan in the form of rain, snow, lakes, or maybe even oceans.

Triton, a moon of Neptune, with an atmosphere of methane and nitrogen, may have pools and seas of liquid nitrogen. No one knows what strange, exciting life-forms have developed on Titan or Triton.

For scientists of the future, our solar system is like a giant research laboratory. It's ripe with the possibilities of amazing discoveries of new and unique forms of life. Such exploration may someday provide the answers to some of the great mysteries of the universe.

Helicopter or Spacecraft?

On Tuesday, August 30, 1977, nineteen-year-old Bob Cray had just finished playing in a football game on Fitch Mountain, east of Healdsburg in northern California.

Mrs. Cray was driving Bob and her three other children home from the game. "Look at those lights in the distance, kids," said Mrs. Cray. They all saw large, round blinking lights over the coastal hills. The largest light was cream colored and the six smaller ones were blue, green, and red.

When the Crays reached the intersection of Highway 101 and Old Redwood Highway, one of the lights seemed to zoom in at them within 40 feet of the road.

As Mrs. Cray drove south on Old Redwood Highway, the road became flooded with light. According to Mrs. Cray, the light was "much brighter than the high beams of a car. It was like the light was in my head." Ten-year-old Jeff had to put his hands over his eyes.

Mrs. Cray described an object about 50 feet in diameter with several windows and two beams of light. Eighteen-year-old Cathy said she saw a face looking at them from one of the windows.

The object was 10 to 20 feet from the car, but the Crays said it felt like they could reach out and touch it. The incident seemed to be happening in slow motion, like in a dream, the Crays recalled.

The strange craft flew off, and the Crays reached the house of Mr. Melville, who saw a bright object in the sky over the local winery, about a half mile away. At about the same time, a woman called the Healdsburg police station to report an unidentified object in the sky.

In his book *Confrontations*, Jacques Vallee investigated the sighting and discovered that the Air National Guard had been conducting maneuvers that night off the coast of Bodega Bay, 40 miles from Healdsburg. Had the Cray family seen the maneuvers and mistaken them for UFOs?

Vallee checked the weather report and found that the temperature that night was in the eighties and visibility was 30 miles. The Air National Guard commander explained that helicopters were used on their maneuvers and that they carried powerful floodlights and dropped bright flares. However, all their exercises were miles offshore, nowhere close to the Healdsburg area.

Could the Crays have seen the helicopter floodlights? The National Guard commander said that on a clear night the floodlights could be seen 100 miles away. The time of the maneuvers coincided with the exact time of the UFO sighting by the Crays.

It is probable that the lights the Crays first saw on Fitch Mountain were the National Guard helicopters many miles away. But that doesn't explain the close encounter with the large, windowed object on Old Redwood Highway!

Did one of the helicopters fly over to Healdsburg and appear near the Crays' car? It's not likely that a helicopter would ignore orders right in the middle of maneuvers and leave its assigned area. Also, the Crays would have recognized a helicopter when they saw one. Even powerful floodlights couldn't disguise the rotor noise and wind that would have blown dust and debris all over the road.

If it wasn't a helicopter, then what was the large windowed craft that the Crays saw near their car? And what did Mr. Melville see flying over the winery, also observed by another woman in town?

Did the Crays, Mr. Melville, and the woman all share a strange UFO hallucination? Did they all see a large military helicopter but fail to recognize it as such? Or did they see hovering above their car a spacecraft that, according to Cathy Cray, was piloted by an intelligent being looking out at them?

Jacques Vallee thinks the Crays told what they believed to be the truth. But what they actually observed in reality is still uncertain.

Helicopter or UFO? What do you think?

The Search for Life

The huge alien spacecraft, escorted by Air Force fighter planes, glides over the nation's capitol. Government leaders and citizens alike watch with a mixture of admiration and fear as the saucer-shaped ship touches down on the grass near the Lincoln Memorial.

After a few minutes, a door slides open and a tall, slender figure walks out, one arm upraised in a friendly greeting. Although the creature walks on two legs, it has four arms and a large, almost swollen, head with huge almond-shaped eyes. The American Secretary of State walks forward to greet the alien and accepts a document carried in one of the creature's arms.

The scene is very peaceful and everyone breathes a sigh of relief. Perhaps the document contains the cure for cancer, or other information that can be used to make the lives of people on Earth happier and healthier.

Time out! This sounds like a scene from an old 1950s science-fiction movie. First contact with extraterrestrial intelligence is not likely to happen this way at all. Read on for a more likely scenario.

Sometime in the near or far future, a NASA radio astronomer will discover a strange signal from another part of the Milky Way galaxy. It may be a beacon to attract attention to that area in the form of a mathematical formula repeated over and over again.

Thomas McDonough, in *The Search for Extraterrestrial Intelligence*, suggests it might be the digits of pi (3.14159) or a series of prime numbers. It would be a signal that only an intelligent civilization could produce.

After the first shock of discovery, the world would finally come to accept the reality of the situation. All telescopes would focus on the area from which the beacon was sent. Eventually, more signals would be discovered and analyzed by the world's scientists. Those who always believed we were alone in the universe would be proved wrong.

Perhaps the signals would begin to tell us

about the aliens and their world. It might take a long time to learn their language and history, but it would finally be accomplished. One day an exchange of information might take place between Earth and the alien civilization!

Such a discovery could change our lives forever. The differences between people on Earth would become insignificant when compared to the differences between Earth people and the aliens. Perhaps contact with intelligent life in another part of the universe could unite our world as never before.

It's a wonderful possibility, and on October 12, 1992, NASA began a 10-year-long project to listen for signals from extraterrestrial civilizations. John Billingham, the scientist heading this High Resolution Microwave Survey (HRMS), stated, "In the first few minutes, more searching was accomplished than in all previous searches combined."

The Deep Space Tracking Station in California's Mojave Desert scans the skies over the Northern Hemisphere. Radio telescopes in Australia sweep the skies over the Southern Hemisphere. The world's largest radio telescope—in Arecibo, Puerto Rico—focuses on 1,000 stars that are within 80 light-years of Earth and are most like our Sun.

Every one of the millions and millions of radio frequencies will be monitored. Powerful computers will lock on to signals that are received, eliminate background noise and any Earth or radio transmissions, and verify the source of the signal. If the signal turns out to be produced by technology and not nature, NASA will announce the discovery to the world. The greatest search in our history has begun. While NASA scientists listen patiently, the whole world waits.

Astronauts and UFOs

"What was it?" exclaimed astronaut Buzz Aldrin just before the moon landing on July 20, 1969.

"What's there? Mission Control calling *Apollo 11*."

"These babies were huge, sir ... enormous ..." said Aldrin. "I'm telling you there are other spacecraft out here.... They're on the moon watching us. ..."

According to Charles Berlitz and William Moore in their book *The Roswell Incident*, this conversation was supposed to have taken place before America's first moon landing. Berlitz and Moore got this material from a source who works with Anglia TV in London, England.

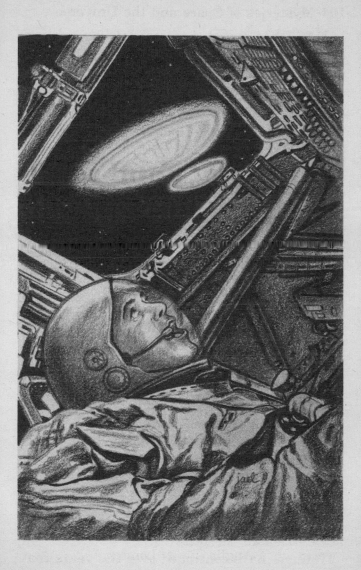

NASA has stated these are falsified conversations. But Maurice Chatelain, author and former chief of NASA Communications for the Apollo lunar missions, believes this dialogue really took place.

Chatelain claims "all Apollo or Gemini flights were followed . . . quite closely by space vehicles of extraterrestrial origin. Every time it occurred, the astronauts informed Mission Control who then ordered absolute silence."

He believes that encounters made by astronauts in space have generally been ignored by NASA and have never reached the public. Berlitz and Moore list a table of astronaut sightings compiled by Chatelain, sightings that raise many questions.

Did Mercury astronaut Cooper in 1963 pick up a voice recording in a language not known on Earth? Did *Gemini 4* astronauts McDivitt and White almost collide with a mysterious silver cylinder over Hawaii and then photograph it? Did *Apollo 8* astronauts Borman, Lovell, and Anders see disk-shaped UFOs as they circled the moon?

Maurice Chatelain thinks so. During the moon landing by *Apollo 11* astronauts, he claims, two spacecraft appeared on the crater rim and Aldrin photographed them, but NASA never released the pictures.

Rumors have continued over the years that

astronauts saw strange formations on the moon's surface that resembled walls, bridges, and even pyramids. Supposedly, even Russian cosmonauts saw arrangements of stones that looked like a runway.

Were the bridges and walls just natural formations of ridges and cliffs? Were the pyramids just illusions and shadows? Was the stone runway just some scattered rocks?

Did these astronauts imagine that they saw formations made by intelligent beings, when in fact they just saw rocks, cliffs, and ridges? No one knows. To this day, the astronauts have kept silent, as has NASA.

There are those who believe our progress into space is being monitored by extraterrestrials. Until the day comes that there is concrete evidence to support the existence of other life, rumors will continue.

What the Future Might Hold

"Welcome to National Airways Space Shuttle Flight 236 to Lunar Base 4 with a six-hour stopover on the Skylab orbiting space station. Please keep your seat belts fastened at all times."

The Kent family was on their way to the moon. Mrs. Kent and her three children, Stacy, Paul, and Shannon, were going to visit Mr. Kent, who worked in a manufacturing module on Lunar Base 4. It was the first trip into space for the children, and they were very excited.

As the rocket blasted off, they kept their eyes to the window. Higher and higher they traveled until they could see the entire United

States and then the whole Northern Hemisphere. Within minutes they were landing at the space station that orbited the Earth, nearly 200 miles above the surface.

"Dad recommended we should eat dinner at the Galaxy Restaurant," said Mom. "During the course of the meal we can watch the Earth revolving beneath us."

"Cool, Mom," said Stacy. "How long will it take for the Earth to make one complete turn?"

"I know, I know," shouted Shannon. "It takes ninety minutes."

"After dinner, let's tour the space station," said Paul. "They check out satellites and launch them from there, and all flights to the Moon and Mars start from there, too!"

"Don't forget that there are manufacturing labs, too, kids," said Mom, "similar to the ones your dad works in on the Moon. Materials and medicines that are difficult to produce on Earth are able to be made in the zero-gravity of space."

After the Kents had dinner and toured the space station, it was time to board their two-day flight to the Moon. Once the spacecraft was under way, the girls watched the Earth for a time and then fell asleep.

Later, the family used their special gravity boots to go to the rest room to wash up for snacks. Food and drinks were served in small

pouches with straws, so they wouldn't float up to the ceiling.

Shannon, who was getting bored, took off her gravity boots and floated around the cabin for a few minutes. Mrs. Kent and a flight attendant finally got her settled. The other children laughed and applauded the antics of their sister, but Mrs. Kent wasn't very pleased.

At last, they docked at Lunar Base 4. John Kent hugged and kissed his wife and children. "Let me show you around the place," he said eagerly.

"The manufacturing modules are next to the chemistry lab and medical labs. We do experimental research as well as production here," explained Dad. "Right now we're testing a type of solar-powered energy satellite and working on an advanced robotic probe for use on Titan, one of Saturn's moons."

"You know, kids, the Moon is full of natural resources," he continued. "We mine titanium and extract minerals from the Moon's surface."

"What about the observatory, Dad?" asked Stacy. "Can we go there?"

"Tomorrow we'll travel to the far side of the Moon that faces away from the Earth, where the lunar observatory is located," answered Dad.

"I can't wait," said Stacy, who wanted to be an astronomer.

Just then Mom spoke up. "I don't know if I'll get used to this day-night cycle."

"Sun for two weeks, then darkness for two weeks," said Dad. "It's strange at first, but you'll get used to it."

He put his arms around his family. "Did you all know that we're pumping enough oxygen on the Moon so that in another few decades there'll be a breathable atmosphere?"

"That's rad, Dad, but when do we get to go to the Mars base?" asked Paul.

"Our base on Mars isn't as advanced as the lunar bases, Paul," answered Dad, "but by the time you're my age, I'll bet you'll be able to take a vacation on Mars!"

"Cool," said Stacy.

"Have I told you all that I'm absolutely thrilled to have you here with me?" Dad said.

This story hasn't happened yet, but scientists believe the chances are good that much of it *will* happen in the future—probably in your lifetime. That's a lot to look forward to!

Glossary

ABRUPT: sudden, unexpected.

AERONAUTICS: the science or art of operating aircraft.

ALTERNATIVE: a choice between two or more things.

ANALYSIS: to study in detail, examine.

ANTICS: fooling around, clowning.

ARTIFICIAL: made by human work in imitation of something natural.

ASTEROID: rocky remains from the formation of the planets billions of years ago.

AXIAL: around or along an imaginary or real straight line on which an object rotates.

BALSA: very lightweight wood.

BEACON: a guiding light or signal.

BARREN: bare, unproductive.

BLEAK: harsh, gloomy.

CAUSALITY: the effect of something always comes after its cause.

COINCIDE: to be exactly alike, to occur at the same time.

COMETS: balls of icy substances such as water, ammonia, methane, dust, and small bits of rocky material with a solid rock center.

CONCLUSIVE: final, decisive.

CONFIRM: establish as true what is doubtful or uncertain.

CONTINENTAL SHELF: the submerged edge of a continent.

COSMIC: relating to the universe.

DEBRIS: wreckage, rubbish.

DENSE: thick, packed tightly.

DEPLETE: to exhaust or drain of energy or funds.

DETECT: to find out, discover the existence of.

DISK, DISC: thin, flat circular object.

DISCREPANCY: difference, disagreement.

DIVERT: turn aside, distract.

DUPLICATE: make an exact copy.

ELONGATION: lengthening.

ENCOUNTER: meet unexpectedly.

EQUIDISTANT: equally distant.

EVOLVE: develop gradually, unfold.
EXCESSIVE: beyond what is usual, too much.
EXTRACT: take out, remove.
EXTRATERRESTRIAL: alien, not of this earth.

FOSSILS: remains of plant or animal life preserved in rock formations.
FUSION: combining of the nuclei of atoms under intense heat to release nuclear energy.

GRAVITY: weight, heaviness.
GREENHOUSE EFFECT: warming of the Earth's atmosphere.

HABITATION: a place in which to live.
HELIOPAUSE: the true edge of the solar system.
HEMISPHERE: one of two halves of the Earth.
HIEROGLYPHICS: pictures or symbols representing words and sounds.
HOAX: fake, trick.

INTERCEPT: stop or interrupt the course of, cut off.
INVERSION: a weather condition in which the air temperature at high altitudes increases instead of decreases.
IRRIGATION: to supply with water.

JUSTIFY: show a reason for something done, explain.

LUNAR: moon, moonlike.

MEGATON: explosive force of a million tons of TNT.

METALLIC: metal-like.

METEORITE: any object that passes through the Earth's atmosphere and reaches the ground.

MILLIMETER: one-thousandth of a meter (.03937 inch).

MODULE: building unit of measurement.

MONITOR: to watch or check on a person or thing.

OORT CLOUD: area in space in which billions of comets orbit around the sun.

ORGANIC: pertaining to living organisms, containing carbon.

ORGANISM: any living thing.

PERSISTENT: refusing to give up, continuing.

PHENOMENON: extraordinary occurrence or experience.

POTENTIAL: possible, undeveloped.

PRECISION: exact, accurate.

PREPOSTEROUS: absurd, ridiculous.

PRIMITIVE: ancient, beginning.

PROBE: explore, investigate.

QUASARS: bright and powerful energy sources located at the center of distant galaxies.

La

Glossary

115

RADAR: electronic device that determines the presence and location of an object.

RADIO FREQUENCY: the number of electromagnetic waves used in the transmission of radio signals.

RECONSTRUCT: rebuild.

REFUGEE: person who flees from home for various reasons to find new shelter.

RESERVOIRS: lakes or ponds in which water is collected and stored for later use.

ROTOR: rotating part of a helicopter.

RUBBLE: wreckage, rubbish.

SALVAGE: rescue, save.

SATELLITE: man-made object put into orbit around the Earth, the Sun, or other heavenly body.

SCENARIO: scene, part of a story or play.

SEVERE: harsh, strict, extreme.

SHIMMER: to shine with an unsteady light.

SINGULARITY: the point at the center of every black hole where the density is so great the laws of physics don't apply in regard to time and space.

STELLAR: relating to stars, composed of stars.

SUBMERGE: place under water.

SUPERNOVA: exploding star 100 million times brighter than the Sun.

SURVEILLANCE: observation.

TAMPER: to interfere with.

TECHNOLOGY: applied science.

TERRAIN: natural ground features.

THERMONUCLEAR: pertaining to nuclear reactions that require extremely high temperatures.

THERMOPHILES: heat-loving bacteria.

THRIVE: grow, flourish.

TRANSPARENT: seen through, clear.

TSUNAMIS: huge tidal waves that are the result of earthquakes or volcanic eruptions.

ULTRAVIOLET: just beyond the violet end of the visible light spectrum.

UNINHABITABLE: not fit to live in.

UNSTABLE: easily upset, changeable.

VERIFY: to prove to be true, check the accuracy of.

VIOLATE: to break, fail to observe.

WARRANT: reason for something, justify.

Bibliography

Books

Asimov, Isaac. *A Choice of Catastrophes*. New York: Simon and Shuster, 1979.

———.*Asimov's Guide to Halley's Comet*. New York: Walker and Company, 1985.

———.*Extraterrestrial Civilizations*. New York: Crown Publishers, Inc., 1979.

———.*How Did We Find Out About Black Holes?* New York: Walker and Company, 1978.

———.*How Did We Find Out About the Speed of Light?* New York: Walker and Company, 1986.

———.*Isaac Asimov's Guide to Earth and Space*. New York: Random House, 1991.

118 Mysteries of Space and the Universe

————.*Please Explain.* New York: Houghton Mifflin Company, 1973.

————.*Quasars, Pulsars, and Black Holes.* Milwaukee, Wis.: Gareth Stevens Publishing, 1988.

Berlitz, Charles, and Moore, William L. *The Roswell Incident.* New York: Grosset and Dunlop, 1980.

Bova, Ben, and Preiss, Byron, eds. *First Contact.* New York: NAL Books, 1990.

Briazack, Norman J., and Mennick, Simon. *The UFO Guidebook.* Secaucus, N.J.: The Citadel Press, 1978.

Close, Frank. *Apocalypse When?* New York: William Morrow and Company, Inc., 1988.

Constable, George, ed. *Comets, Asteroids, and Meteorites.* Alexandria, Va.: Time-Life Books, 1990.

————.*Cosmic Mysteries.* Alexandria, Va.: Time-Life Books, 1990.

————.*Life Search.* Alexandria, Va.: Time-Life Books, 1988.

Delgado, Pat, and Andrews, Colin. *Circular Evidence.* London: Bloombury Publishing, 1989.

Evans, Barry. *The Wrong-Way Comet and Other Mysteries of Our Solar System.* Blue Ridge Summit, Pa.: Tab Books, 1992.

Lewis, Richard S. *Space in the 21st Century.* New York: Columbia University Press, 1990.

McDonough, Thomas R. *Space—The Next Twenty-five Years.* New York: John Wiley and Sons, Inc., 1987.

——.*The Search for Extraterrestrial Intelligence.* New York: John Wiley and Sons, Inc., 1987.

Parker, Barry. *Cosmic Time Travel.* New York: Plenum Press, 1991.

Raintree Publishing Staff. *Astronomy.* Milwaukee, Wis.: Raintree Publishers, 1988.

Sagan, Carl, and Page, Thornton. *UFOs—A Scientific Debate.* New York: W. W. Norton and Company, 1972.

Sheehan, William. *Worlds in the Sky.* Tucson, Ariz.: The University of Arizona Press, 1992.

Spencer, John, and Evans, Hilary. *Phenomenon—Forty Years of Flying Saucers.* New York: Avon Books, 1988.

Story, Ronald D. *Sightings.* New York: William Morrow and Company, 1981.

Trefil, James. *The Dark Side of the Universe.* New York: Charles Scribner's Sons, 1988.

Vallee, Jacques. *Confrontations.* New York: Ballantine Books, 1990.

————.*Revelations*. New York: Ballantine Books, 1991.

Periodicals

Beck, Melinda, and Glick, Daniel. "And If the Comet Misses." *Newsweek*, 23 November 1992.

Begley, Sharon. "The Science of Doom." *Newsweek*, 23 November 1992.

Coleman, Jim. "A Puzzle Over the Centuries." *Los Angeles Times*, 22 October 1985.

Dietrich, Bill. "Scientists Start Star Search for Intelligent Life." *Inland Valley Daily Bulletin*, 14 October 1992.

Dye, Lee. "NASA Holds Its Breath and Listens for Other Worlds." *Los Angeles Times*, 7 October 1992.

Easterbrook, Gregg. "Return of the Glaciers." *Newsweek*, 23 November 1992.

Haldin, Ken. "A Twice in a Lifetime Experience for Some." *Los Angeles Times,* 22 October 1985.